Mom and Dad Are Always So Busy

Written by B. Annye Rothenberg, Ph.D.
Child & Parent Psychologist

Illustrated by
Bonnie Bright

REDWOOD CITY, CALIFORNIA

DEDICATION

To the many parents who do all they can – and then even more – to raise their children well. ALMOST every minute of parenting will have been worth it.

And to my adult son, Bret, who is my most favorite person in the world!

—B.A.R.

Text copyright © 2019 by B. Annye Rothenberg
Illustrations copyright © 2019 by Bonnie Bright

All rights reserved. No part of this book may be reproduced, stored in a retrieval system, or transmitted in any form by any means, electronic, mechanical, photocopy, recording or otherwise, without express written permission from the publisher, except for the inclusion of brief quotations in a review.

Library of Congress Control Number: 2018938191

ISBN: 978-0-9790420-7-2 (pbk.)

Printed in Hong Kong   First printing January 2019
10 9 8 7 6 5 4 3 2 1

Published by
PERFECTING PARENTING PRESS
REDWOOD CITY, CALIFORNIA
www.PerfectingParentingPress.com

To order by phone, call:
(810) 388-9500 (M-F 9-5 ET)
For other questions, call:
(650) 275-3809 (M-F 8-5 PT)

Children's book in collaboration with
SuAnn and Kevin Kiser
Palo Alto, California

Parents' manual final editing
Kevin and SuAnn Kiser
Palo Alto, California

Book design by
Cathleen O'Brien
San Francisco, California

About the Cover

These busy parents have lots of demands on them. They're trying to find more time to be with their three children, but the children don't feel it's enough. (In this book, there are practical solutions for everyone in the family.)

To parents *(and parenting guidance professionals):*

• WHAT'S IN THIS BOOK FOR CHILDREN AND FOR PARENTS •

This eighth book in a series focuses on busy families, particularly those with two full-time working parents. It's for families with children from four to nine years old.

Over the last ten to 15 years, it's become increasingly common for both parents to be in the workforce. **When both parents work, parenting seems to be harder.**

This book has been written to guide you in a very practical way to know how to do a good job in parenting while meeting the expectations of your work. You'll find two parts to this book: a story for children and a guidance section for parents.

The story for children explains the perspective of the siblings, *Brandon who is nine years old, Chloe who is seven years old, and Oliver who is four years old,* as they talk together about their parents. The children then express their concerns to their parents. Together, the whole family finds ways to better meet more of all their needs. This beautifully illustrated story has enough real life experiences and suggestions to make it an easily understandable and useful experience.

The parent guidance section covers: *how to feel close to your children even when you're busy,* how to help them know how much they matter to you, *how to talk to them about their problems, and what warning signs to look for so you can head off developing difficulties.* This parent section also includes: what to expect of your four- to nine-year-olds and what are good routines; as well as important *parenting basics* including *the newest consequences, and important values including how to choose good friends.* (See the Table of Contents on page 26 for all the topics that are included.)

The parent guidance section will help you gain important skills. *Make sure you read only one topic at a time because there's much to absorb.* This book is all about enhancing the enjoyment of family life for ourselves and our kids and preparing our children for a good future.

— **Annye Rothenberg, Ph.D., Child & Parent Psychologist**

Dr. Annye Rothenberg's **Mom and Dad Are Always So Busy** book *is an excellent read for working parents. It provides many practical pointers that enable parents to be more successful in the tug-of-war between the demands of work and the needs of the children. This book has guidelines for many typical situations, including how to spend quality time with your children. It will definitely be very useful to me as a working parent.*

— Shubhda Roy, mother of an eight-year-old son and in Research IT, Foster City, CA

Dr. Rothenberg's newest book, **Mom and Dad Are Always So Busy**, *offers much help to busy families looking to find ways to stay connected to each other. The story for children and parents to read together has a lighthearted tone, yet delivers an important message. In addition, the parent guidance section has a great deal of valuable advice for parents which they will find especially useful.*

— Patrice Warto and Carla Murray, Pre-Kindergarten Teachers and mothers, Serendipity Preschool, San Mateo, CA

"Brandon, do you want to play with Oliver and me?" asked my sister Chloe.

"Not right now," I said. "I'm too upset."

"Why?" asked Oliver.

"Because Mom promised to watch the video I made of the squirrel in our backyard, but then someone from work called and she got so busy she forgot about me...again."

"Mom and Dad are always too busy," said Chloe.

"If they're not on their phones or computers," I said, "they're doing chores."

"And they keep saying 'hurry up' and making us rush," said Oliver. "It makes me mad...and sometimes sad."

"When the time is just right," I said, "I think we should tell Mom and Dad how we all feel."

"Me too," said Chloe.

"Me three," said Oliver.

That night after dinner I asked Dad, "Can we work on my science project now? You promised we could do it tonight."

"Sure," said Dad. Then his phone rang. "It's my client. Give me a minute, Brandon." He walked down the hall and into his office to take the call.

Later Mom asked, "How are you doing on your science project, Brandon?"

"Not very well," I grumbled. "Dad was supposed to help me, but he's still on his phone."

"What's a science project?" asked Oliver.

"I'm showing how water turns into ice," I said.

"Just put it in the freezer!" said Oliver.

"Not little ice cubes," I said, "really big ice, like glaciers and icebergs."

"Use a really **big** freezer!" said Oliver.

"Dad and I were going to make a model glacier," I said, "but Dad forgot about me."

"Maybe your science project should be to freeze Mom's and Dad's phones," said Chloe.

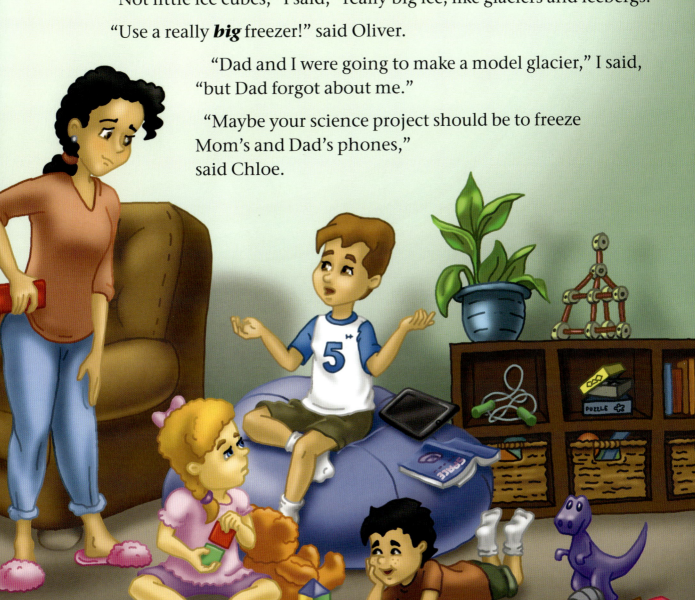

When Dad came back into the room, he said, "It looks like I have some extra work tonight. How about we do your science project tomorrow night?"

"Dad, I know you're busy," I said, "but my science project is important too, and I thought when you make a promise, you're supposed to keep it."

"You're right, Brandon," said Dad. "I promised you first. I'll tell my client that I'll get back to him later."

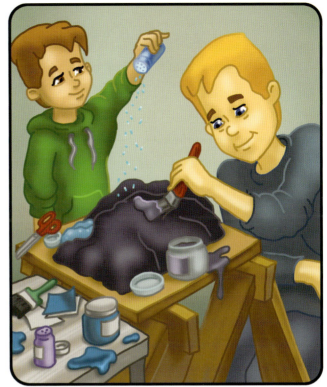

Dad and I built a model glacier and painted it blue and purple. Then we showed everyone.

"That's beautiful!" said Mom.

"I like the sparkles!" Chloe said.

"It won't fit in the freezer," said Oliver.

During breakfast on Saturday, I thought the time was just right to bring up how we felt, so I said, "Mom, Dad...do you still love Oliver and Chloe and me?"

"Of course!" said Mom.

"More than anything!" said Dad. "Why do you ask that?"

"Because it seems like you never have enough time for us," I said, "even when you're at home."

"That doesn't mean we don't love you," said Dad.

"We're just so busy," said Mom.

"The other day, my teacher told the class that you can tell what people care about most by what they spend the most time doing," I said. "It seems like you care more about work and everyone else than about us."

"Is that how you all feel?" Dad asked.

We all nodded.

"We wish you would spend more time with us," I said.

"And that you wouldn't tell us to hurry up so much," said Oliver.

"We want you to eat dinner with us more often," I said.

"And to read us separate bedtime stories," said Chloe.

"We need a family meeting to discuss all those things," said Mom.

"Let's do that tonight," said Dad. "Right now, how about we all do something fun together!"

"Can we go to the zoo?" I asked.

"With no calls or texts?" asked Chloe.

"And pet the lions?" asked Oliver.

"Phones for emergencies only," said Mom.

"We promise!" said Dad. "Except for petting the lions."

"Good call," I whispered to Dad.

"Elephants!" shouted Oliver, when we got to the zoo.

"Look at that!" said Dad. "Mama is giving Baby a shower."

The baby elephant shook its head and flung water on the mama. "Now Baby is giving Mama a shower!" said Chloe.

Mom's phone buzzed. "It could be an emergency," she said. "You go ahead, I'll catch up."

"We'll wait," I said.

"I don't think **telling** Mom and Dad how we feel and what we want was enough," said Chloe.

"Let's make up stories about the zoo animals so we can **show** them too," I said.

"Oh boy!" shouted Oliver. "Show and Tell!"

When Mom hung up, we all looked at her.

"It wasn't an emergency after all," she said.

We went to the beaver dam. "If Beaver Dad had a phone," I said, "the kids wouldn't learn how to build new dams, and soon none of the beavers would have a place to live."

"I guess they wouldn't have to clean their rooms, then," said Dad.

At the lion compound, Chloe said, "If Mom and Dad Lion had jobs, they would never have time to hunt for food, so the lion family would have to eat grass."

"Yum!" said Mom. "Probably tastes like fresh spinach!"

At the monkey cages, Oliver said, "If those monkeys had tablets, they would watch cat videos all day and never do anything together!"

"Hmmm..." said Dad, "maybe Mom and I should have less work and phone time when it's family time with you little monkeys." He ruffled Oliver's hair and Oliver jumped up and down and screeched like a monkey.

Later, at the family meeting, Mom asked, "Any ideas how we can have more family time?"

"We could help you and Dad out more around the house," I said, "so that you would have more time to spend with us after the chores."

"And **during** the chores too!" said Dad.

"I can help Mom fold clothes," said Chloe, "and help Dad unpack groceries."

"I can help Dad wash the dishes," I said, "and help Mom sweep the floor."

"I can pick up dust bunnies!" said Oliver.

"Sounds great," said Mom, "if you are sure you will help every day…"

"We will!" I said.

"We promise!" said Chloe. Oliver nodded.

"Any other ideas?" asked Dad.

"Maybe if we get up earlier, we won't have to rush," said Oliver.

"That could work, if you kids get to bed earlier too," said Mom, "**and** if you stay in your rooms and don't keep calling for us after we say goodnight."

"How about eating dinner together more often?" I asked.

"We can do that," said Dad, "except when Mom or I have to work late, or I'm traveling for business."

"When Dad's away," said Mom, "we could have a video conference dinner!"

"Just don't ask me to pass the peas," said Dad.

We all laughed.

"Would you read each of us separate bedtime stories?" asked Chloe.

"I'm old enough to read to myself," I said.

"Then Dad and I could each read different stories to Chloe and Oliver," said Mom, "and chat with Brandon at his bedtime."

"And since **we're** not allowed to have screen time on weekdays," I said, "could you wait to use your phones until after we go to bed?"

"These are all great ideas," said Dad.

"Let's create a plan together," said Mom.

Our new plan showed when we would do chores and who we would do them with, as well as when we would have family time together. Everyone promised to follow it.

On Sunday, we followed the plan. All the chores got done, we ate dinner together, and went to bed early. Mom and Dad read Oliver and Chloe different bedtime stories, while I read to myself. I even got to chat with Mom and Dad. We were all happy with the new plan.

On Monday, during family time, Dad's and Mom's phones kept buzzing until they answered them. Oliver and Chloe and I were disappointed. It looked like the plan might not work after all.

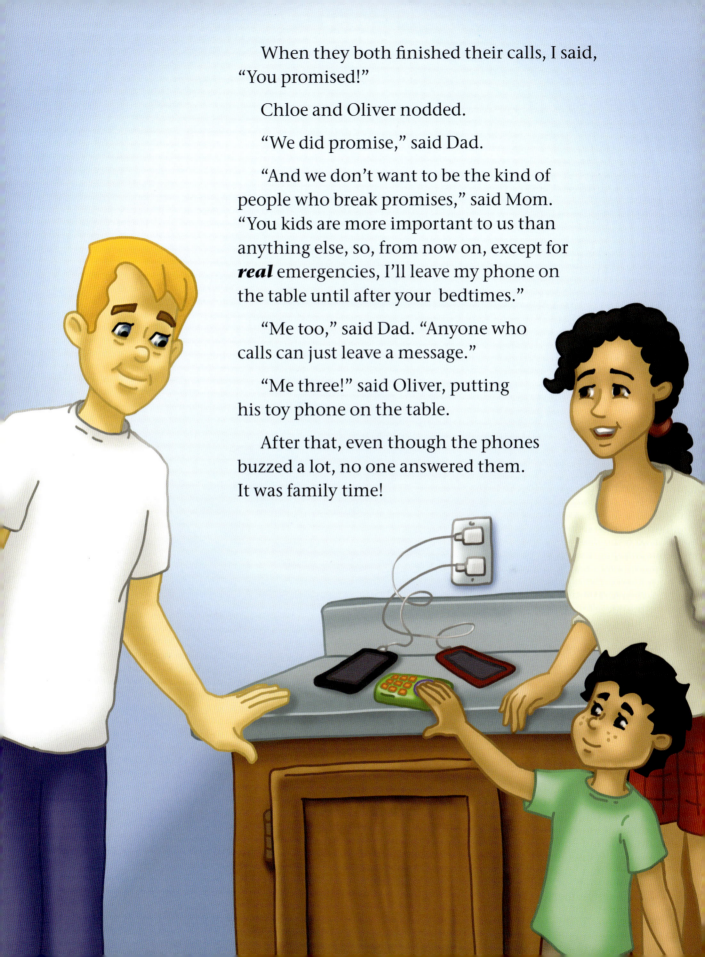

When they both finished their calls, I said, "You promised!"

Chloe and Oliver nodded.

"We did promise," said Dad.

"And we don't want to be the kind of people who break promises," said Mom. "You kids are more important to us than anything else, so, from now on, except for **real** emergencies, I'll leave my phone on the table until after your bedtimes."

"Me too," said Dad. "Anyone who calls can just leave a message."

"Me three!" said Oliver, putting his toy phone on the table.

After that, even though the phones buzzed a lot, no one answered them. It was family time!

When our chores were all finished, I showed everyone the video I made of our backyard squirrel fighting with a crow over a nut.

"Those sure are silly animals," Mom said.

"If they had phones," I said, "they could have ordered a pizza to share!"

Everyone laughed.

Just then someone's phone started buzzing, but nobody seemed to care. We just laughed even harder.

TABLE OF CONTENTS

WHAT'S IN THIS BOOK FOR PARENTS AND CHILDREN......3

A GUIDANCE SECTION FOR PARENTS: INTRODUCTION......26

SECTION ONE: HOW YOUR CHILDREN CAN FEEL UNDERSTOOD AND CLOSE TO YOU EVEN THOUGH YOU ARE BUSY......27
- The Special Influence of Parents on Their Children......27
- Talking With Your Children About Why You're Busy......27
- When You've Been Especially Unavailable to Your Kids......28
- Making Sure Your Children Feel They Matter to You When You're With Them......28
- Warning Signs to Watch For......29
- Helping Your Children Talk About Any of Their Problems......30
- Why Children Need One-On-One Time with You and How to Find That Time......30

SECTION TWO: REASONABLE EXPECTATIONS AND ROUTINES FOR YOUR FOUR- TO NINE-YEAR-OLDS......31
- Expectations and Routines for Four- to Nine-Year-Olds......31
  - Waking-up and Getting Ready......31
  - Before Leaving Home......32
  - After School and Until Just Before Bedtime......32
  - Bedtime and Sleep Routines......33
- Have Your Four- to Nine-Year-Olds Learn to Do What's Age-Appropriate...33
- What Do You and Your Children Need from Each Other at the End of the Day......34

SECTION THREE: USEFUL PARENTING BASICS......35
1. Try Not to Give Your Children Too Much Say or Too Much Control—Too Young......35
2. Consequences: Which to Avoid, Which to Keep, and Two NEW Ones...36
3. What To Do About Your Children's Screen Time......38
4. Dealing With Your Children's Homework......39
5. Don't Let Your Children Stay Up Too Late—Have a Set Bedtime......39
6. How to See for Yourself What Your Children Are Experiencing at School......40
7. Consider What Your Children's Teachers Tell You......40

SECTION FOUR: FINDING THE RIGHT SCHOOL AND THE RIGHT WORK SCHEDULE FOR YOUR FAMILY......41
- Finding Quality Schools and After-School Care......41
- Other Work Schedules That Can Ease Your Parenting......41

SECTION FIVE: IMPORTANT VALUES WE WANT TO TEACH OUR CHILDREN AND HOW TO DO IT......42
1. How Our Kids Can Accept That They Can't Have Everything They Want......42
2. Helping Our Children Deal with Their Frustration and Anger......44
3. Teach Your Children How to Choose Good Friends and to Be a Good Friend......44
4. How Your Kids Can Learn to Keep Their Word and Be Honest......45

CONCLUSION: WHAT'S DIFFERENT NOW FOR BOTH MOMS AND DADS?......46

A GUIDANCE SECTION FOR PARENTS

• INTRODUCTION •

This parenting guidance section is for busy working parents with four- to nine-year-old children. Working full-time while parenting is very challenging. There is a busyness to the family that requires a lot of juggling. We try solutions and then discard them. We worry about how we're doing at work and usually even more about how our children are doing.

The information in this book can help you to make better decisions about your children and how to more successfully combine being in the workforce *while* parenting. The emphasis is on how to handle the competing demands and the limited time you have to meet those demands. This book will help you make the most of your time with your children. *Because you only get to raise your kids once, this guidance section helps you know what to emphasize when your children are young, so you don't have regrets later in life.*

The purpose of both parts of this book (the children's story *and* the parent guidance section) is to help you and your children see one another's perspectives, and to help all of you find ways to make some important improvements in your life together.

• SECTION ONE •
HOW YOUR CHILDREN CAN FEEL UNDERSTOOD AND CLOSE TO YOU EVEN THOUGH YOU ARE BUSY

The Special Influence of Parents on Their Children

As parents, we have the greatest impact on our children, even though we often have fewer hours with them than their teachers and other caregivers do. Part of the reason we are the most important people to our kids is that we have a loving lifelong commitment to them and we care more about them than anyone else does. We would do anything possible for them. That is what defines parents. In contrast, teachers have **many** children who are their focus—*different children every year. Parents' huge impact comes from caring so deeply about who our children are now, and what we need to do to guide them, always with an eye to what is best for them currently and in the future.*

We want to teach our children our most important values and help them become happy people who are successful in finding their own interests and skills. We want them to know how to form and maintain meaningful and caring relationships with others. Our goal is for them to have satisfying and productive lives.

When our children are adults, most of us hope that they will choose to have children of their own. We also hope that they will have learned from us that there are many ways to have enough time to raise and enjoy their children while also working and gaining satisfaction from their chosen career.

Talking With Your Children About Why You're Busy

It's helpful to our children when we explain why we're so busy. Many of our children experience us as busy people—typically because work takes a lot of our time and often leaves us with too much to do when we get home.

When it's your job that is keeping you busy, you can help your children understand by explaining that nearly *everyone needs to have a job.* Tell them that people work so they can earn money to pay for the things we all need and want, such as our home, food, clothes, toys, books, activities, and vacations. **This is why everybody needs to** *learn a lot about something that's interesting to them—something that can become their job when they're grown-up.* This is part of the reason children go to school and have a lot to learn, just like Mom and Dad did. It's important to encourage your child to ask you any questions or make any comments as you try to explain why you're busy.

When you are working long hours or have to bring work home, you can explain to your children that there are many times when there's more work to do than there is time in the workday. This may be because something has to be re-done, colleagues are out sick or on vacation, or customers need your help. Tell them that sometimes you may have to stay longer at work or bring work home to do after they go to sleep.

Your children might also ask why some moms (or dads) don't work, or ask why you can't stay home to be with them more. There are many ways to answer this. *The two most common ways are about how much studying it took to learn how to do your job—one that you like a lot.* You want to keep doing this work so you need to learn the newest skills to do your job well. *The other reason is about earning enough money to care for your family. It could be both reasons.* If that's not enough for them, also tell them that some moms don't work because they haven't found the kind of job that they would really like to do. Some don't work because they have many kids and it's too hard to be in the workforce and manage everyone's schedule. And, sometimes parents believe that mom should only take on the responsibility of being moms like their mothers did.

It's important to tell them something about the conflict you experience because you want to be at home with them **and** you want to do the work that you enjoy. This can be useful to help them understand the kinds of tugs and pulls that you experience and that they may experience when they're older. *Encourage your children to ask you anything they want to know about what you do at work, why you like your work, and how your work helps others.* Try to take them to your workplace on occasion, so they get a first-hand feel for where you go, what you do, and the people you spend time with. This helps your kids be more interested when you talk about your work.

Let them know that almost everyone wants to have children to love, take care of, be with, teach, and do fun things with. Make sure to tell them that moms and dads try very hard to have enough time to be with their children. And that all parents try to find good, loving people like childcare providers, teachers, coaches, etc. to take care of them when parents can't be with them.

Make sure you tell your children how important they are to you, how much you love them and want to be with them, and how you think about them a lot even when you're working. Consider leaving a voice or text message, email or FAX for them, so when they're home, they can hear or see that you meant what you said. They'll enjoy getting these messages even when you're all together at home at the end of the day.

Tell your kids that you know that sometimes you're way too busy so you may not notice when they're not getting enough of your attention. Explain that you want them to let you know when they feel they need more time with you so they don't feel ignored, sad, or angry. *Help them choose a simple phrase they can use to tell you what they need such as: "I need some time with you," or "There's something I have to tell you," or "When are you going to be done?"* When they say any of these things to you, try to make yourself available *very soon*. You could ask them to work with you on the chore you're doing so you can talk to them while you work together or so you'll be available to them sooner. *Expect to have to remind your children that you want them to tell you if they feel ignored. We don't want our children to just give up on having our attention.*

When You've Been Especially Unavailable to Your Kids

On days that your children won't see you in the morning *and* in the evening, arrange a telephone time with them. *It's even better if you can see each other by using Skype or FaceTime. This helps your children feel that they are important to you because you make time for them every day.*

When you haven't seen your children for a few days or more, they may not have much to say, so help get the conversation started by telling them something about your day that they might find interesting. If your spouse has been with your children, ask him or her what has been going on with the children in the last few days so you can ask your kids something meaningful to them.

When you've been working long hours or traveling for more than a day or two, *try to take off some extra time from work to spend with your children.* Use this time to take them out for a walk, or to see something interesting in town, or volunteer for a few hours in their classrooms. *It's*

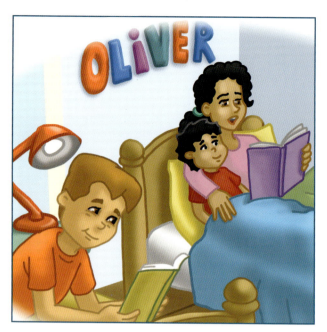

one thing to say you wish you had more time with them. It means much more to them when you make it happen.

Try not to let your children down. That happens a lot when we don't keep our promises. *Their sense of self and their confidence are still developing and can be affected positively or negatively by how we maintain contact with them and* how we keep *or* don't keep our promises.

Making Sure Your Children Feel They Matter to You When You're With Them

What bothers many of our children the most about our being busy is that when we're with them, we often are still preoccupied with other things. They may feel that other people and other things are more important to us than they are. It can seem to children that everyone else is more important to us including the delivery man or the neighbors who stop by to chat. *As parents, we don't feel that way, and we don't want our children to think that's true. So what should we do about it?*

When we've been apart from our children all day, it's very important that our reconnection with them be our highest priority. So when your time with your children is being interrupted by someone not in your family, you need to tell that person, "I'm spending time with my child right now, so I'll have to get back to you." Make sure that your child hears you say that or that you tell him* what you just said to that person because *this helps your child feel that he is very important to you—that he matters.* Telling

---

To avoid the awkwardness of "he or she," this book will use alternating genders topic by topic.

your child to give you 'two minutes' so you can deal with the interrupter right now is likely insulting to him and conveys the message that he's not as important to you as the interrupter is.

Some of our children tell us about how this makes them feel, but *many* children won't speak up because they don't want to hear our excuses again, or be reminded where they are in our hierarchy. ***And if this happens a lot, their feelings of being 'less than' are felt more and more deeply.*** Some of your children may handle your work and home schedule just fine, and others may be very negatively affected. This is because each of our children's personalities and needs can be very different.

Of course, no parent wants to make their child feel less important. We often are torn by our desire to be with our children and our desire to be successful at work. We don't want to be viewed as 'unavailable' when so many of our colleagues are willing to work 'after hours.' This is an important and difficult choice **you'll have to make.** Remember though, **children are far more emotionally impacted than adults, such as your colleagues, about where they are in your hierarchy.**

When our children feel they aren't important enough to us, it can negatively impact their self-esteem, their confidence, and their closeness with us. They may find other ways and situations in which they can be noticed and feel important. Children handle self-esteem and confidence issues in many different ways. Some children handle it more positively by putting all their energy into sports, academics, or other interests. **Some put their energy into misbehavior, which results in their getting negative attention from us and/or from their teachers.** Others just become anxious, sad, angry, or less self-confident.

Warning Signs to Watch For

The following Warning Signs are worth watching for in our children's behavior, so we know when they need more help or attention:
- *Frequent anger and arguing* with you, ignoring you, refusal to do what you ask, tantrums and problems calming down.
- *Frequent sadness*, loss of interest in activities and people.
- Lots of *separation anxiety*, other worries, and fears.
- *Acting up at school*, such as being a class clown or a class bully, and frequently not doing what the teacher asks.
- *Stealing, lying, leading others into poor behavior.*

If you see these types of behaviors in any of your children, talk with them. Discuss their behavior with other adults who spend time with them, especially their teachers. Talk to your children about what's going on in their time away from you. Notice how available you are to them when you're with them. ***See whether spending more time with them helps.*** Read the section (see page 30) about one-on-one time so you can set up predictable times to help your child feel more important to you. ***And during your individual time with him,*** help him talk to you about his problems (see page 30). If you see no improvement after a month, talk to your child's teacher and pediatrician to help you find the right referral sources to help him.

With the best of intentions, we try to meet our children's needs **and** the demands of our job. However, **unless we are willing to draw some clear and consistent boundaries that enable us to meet our children's needs,** we will too frequently go back and forth trying to meet the demands of our kids and our job. Then we will likely feel frustrated, stressed, and disappointed in ourselves because we can't do both well enough. *If you can draw the 'line' after your normal working hours, and focus on your children until their bedtime. Below are some ideas that can help.*

When you're with your children—before and after school, evenings and weekends—be fully with them. During those times, your family needs to come first. When you have more than two children, see how you and your spouse can divide your time among your children. Consider your and their interests. ***Your children's closeness to you comes from how you spend time together when you're with them.*** Try to find a current interest of his **and** yours that you can build on. Examples are wide-ranging such as a sport you're both interested in, a project you both want to work on such as cooking, doing crafts, learning how plumbing or other things work, exploring/reading about a topic like how to take care of the baby or toddler in your family, how the body works, learning about dinosaurs or space travel, discussing a book you've read together, or ***talking about experiences you had as a child that your child might be interested in.*** These things can be enjoyable and very satisfying for each of you. At different childhood stages, you and your spouse may become closer to one or another of your children as you find yourself sharing more common interests.

When you tell any of your children about your day, it not only models how they can share their day with you, it also gives them the opportunity and desire to tell you about their day and to confide in you. Your conversations with, playing with, and working alongside your children make them feel better about themselves, encourages sharing between you, and enables you to teach your values and the important life skills to them.

There is so much we need to teach our children during our time with them. We want that time to have many meaningful and loving moments. *If we can set firmer limits on our work during these important child-rearing years, we can decrease the stress that comes from competing demands between family time and everything else.* Doing this will leave us with fewer future regrets about the way we helped our children when they needed us.

Helping Your Children Talk About Any of Their Problems

Being able to help your children with their problems is a very useful and meaningful experience for us as parents *and* for our children. *Be sure to tell your children that they can tell you about anything that's bothering them. To really mean what you say, it's most beneficial in your relationship with your children that at least one parent be home well before bedtime so there can be this important unwinding time together.* We want to know what's happening in our children's lives and being together in the evening is necessary to this process.

If your child doesn't usually share anything with you, then start a conversation by telling her something fun or interesting about your day, or even about a problem you had—although not a big problem. That makes it easier for her to share her day with you. *It can be very useful if your child seems to have something troublesome on her mind to say to your child,* "It seems as if something is bothering you." Show that you're interested in the details. *Be empathetic (e.g., "Of course, you're bothered about that." or "It sounds like that made you really unhappy (angry, etc.)". Being empathetic encourages your children to tell you the whole story.* Give her enough time to tell you a lot about her problem. *Try hard not to move toward giving her advice. Your responses to what she's saying should enable her to talk more and more about what's bothering her.* Kids usually don't want us to offer advice before they tell us everything about their problem. After she's finished her story (*if* you feel she could answer this question), ask her if she's had any ideas so far for what she can do next.

If your child has no ideas of how to solve her problem, then ask her *if she wants your suggestion. If she says no, then let it go—for now.* If she says yes, *then propose your suggestion with some humility,* "I'm not sure this will work for you…" or "What do you think about…?" or "It's okay if you don't like this idea…" If she doesn't like your idea, she may come up with something better, then or later. *Encourage her to tell you why she thinks your idea won't work for her.* Then you and your child could brainstorm some other possible ideas for this situation until she feels that she has something she could try. *This approach to her problems can help her feel understood and cared about. This is usually what your children want from you.*

Most of us want to tell our children how to solve their problems, and many of us will keep doing that. (If that method seems to be what your child wants, then continue to give her advice.)

However, most children only want our emotional support and encouragement so they can come up with their own possible solutions. And because we want them to become problem solvers, be cautious about going from listening to her problem to immediately telling her how she should solve it. She's not you, and you're not her, and you don't know what she faces at school, etc., so you don't know what really will work for her. And if you later ask her if she used your advice, she may feel uncomfortable because she didn't use it *or* because it didn't work. *So don't ask her that question.* Follow up with her a few days later to see if she has thought more about what she might do or has she tried anything yet to deal with what was troubling her.

You are exactly the right person for your children to share their problems with and for you to offer them your support and encouragement as they learn how to solve their problems.

Why Children Need One-On-One Time With You and How to Find That Time

Since we don't have much free time, it's common to use the time we have *to do all of our activities together as a family* (such as shopping, eating out, walks, movies, museums, etc.). *There is another kind of time that is of great importance—one-on-one time* (that is, one parent with one child for a period of uninterrupted togetherness). This time has so much value because it's a great way to get close to your child. *Having one-on-one time once a week has many benefits. This special time shows your child that you want to be with him just because you like his company, and not because you need him to do something.*

Most children feel especially cherished and valued when they have one-on-one time, but not when it's interrupted by others. One-on-one time builds high self-esteem and confidence. Children also become more willing to do the things that we need to ask them to do.

Here's how to do one-on-one time. It's very easy when you have just one or two children. With two kids, one parent can take one child while the other parent takes the other child. When you have more than two children, each one still needs weekly one-on-one time but it doesn't need to be with both parents. As the weekend begins, a parent can have one-on-one time with one of the kids while the other parent spends time with all the rest of the kids. Then as the weekend goes on, make sure there's one-on-one time for each child by either parent. The only kids who don't need one-on-one time are the under-two-year-olds who get a great deal of one-on-one time due to their need for much one-on-one child care.

This uninterrupted time together could be as little as a half-hour, or longer when possible, so it need not take much of your weekend. It could be a walk, a visit to the pond, a stop at a construction site, or someplace for a snack. It should be something you and your child **both** want to do; **not just what your child wants.** (This helps your child learn about compromising.) *Going someplace where you'll likely run into other people that you know is not a good choice for one-on-one time.* One-on-one time can also be at home when only you and one of your children will be there. *This is a very important activity that truly is worth your time.*

• SECTION TWO •
REASONABLE EXPECTATIONS AND ROUTINES FOR YOUR FOUR- TO NINE-YEAR-OLDS

Expectations and Routines for Four- to Nine-Year-Olds

It's important to know what to expect of our children. **We don't want to baby them** and inadvertently make them **less** independent or competent. We may be doing too much for them if we often have to rush them. On the other hand, **we don't want to ask so much of them that they are stressed.**

Here's what we can realistically expect our four- to nine-year-olds to be able to do as long as we encourage them using reasonable routines:

Waking-up and Getting Ready

• *Children should wake-up easily in the morning, assuming that they didn't go to sleep too late. If we have to wake them in the morning, it means they haven't had enough sleep. Enough sleep is essential because they are still growing and developing. Adjust their bedtimes to be earlier so they can get the 10-11 hours of sleep they need.* (Try moving their bedtimes about 15 minutes earlier every few nights until they are able to wake-up on their own.)

• *Children six years old and older* should know everything they have to do before going to school each morning, and they should be able to do those things without constant nagging. *Four- and five-year-olds, however, need you to help them with all of the morning routines because some of the routines are too difficult and because they tend to get distracted.*

To facilitate this, **help your six- to nine-year-olds make a list of their morning tasks, in an order that they choose and that also works for you.** (You can write the list with little diagrams for the younger ones). If we impose our list of tasks on our six- to nine-year-olds, they're likely to be resistant to doing those things.

To set them up for success, have your **elementary school-age kids** guess how long each morning task will take and **then time them**. Have them write the **actual times** on their list. Your older kids can join you in figuring out what time to get started in the morning. Most kids will find this interesting. Doing this guessing and timing on a non-rushed weekend day will likely work best.

• Four- to nine-year-olds should be able to choose their own clean, weather-appropriate clothes and six- to nine-year-olds should be able to fully dress themselves.

Consider having your *four- and five-year-olds* dress near you in the kitchen or in your bedroom so you can help them dress and model 'keeping on task.' Try to leave enough time so that every minute before school doesn't require you to remind or rush them.

• Children will get through their morning routine more willingly and with less nagging when they know that if they stay focused and complete their list, they'll get some free time before they leave for school. (Try to aim for about 15 minutes of free time.) Screen time activities should not be a free-time option before school because kids find these too difficult to stop.

• Pre-K to third grade children need to know each day's

schedule including who will be taking them from place to place and when. (Children can benefit from having this written or drawn on a calendar hanging in their bedroom or in the kitchen.)

Before Leaving Home

• Children should leave their things in a reasonably organized manner, including putting dirty clothes where they belong, playthings put away except for those few projects that we allow our kids to leave out, and beds made unless you don't make your own bed. (If we don't do it, they can't be expected to.)

• Children should pack everything they need in their backpack. It's best to have most of this done the night before. Four- to five-year-olds will need you to check that they have everything they need in their backpack including their lunch. Older children may still need reminders.

After School and Until Just Before Bedtime

• *After school, kids need a snack and some playtime followed by homework. Many kids will get all of this in their full-day pre-K or in their after-school care.* Otherwise, parents or other caregivers need to provide these at home.

• Children need some free time in the afternoon and evening, although there may be some days when they have scheduled after-school activities. *We want our kids to have some special interest activities, but these shouldn't fill up all of their after-school hours, even when our kids insist on lots of scheduled activities. This is because our children still need time with us.* Activities our kids may be interested in include sports, music, art, science, dance, second languages, and many other possibilities. Many after-school childcare programs now offer some of these special interest activities.

• *Playdates are worth encouraging. They offer another valuable type of socializing for kids who have been in groups all day.* When your child is in group care, and something isn't going well with her peers, she typically can find someone else to play with. *However, with playdates, your child has to learn more about turn-taking, compromise, and even empathy because the visiting child will be the only one to play with.* (Playdates probably will need to be on the weekends and are usually about two hours long for younger kids. As kids get older, playdates can be longer or turned into 'outings.')

• *At least an hour a day of heart-pounding exercise is very important for all kids.* If your kids don't get that at recess or PE, or if they are naturally sedentary, then look for ways to add exercise into your family's time together. Doing fun, outdoor activities as a family will help your children develop a positive attitude toward exercise. Consider having the family play ball, take walks to the park, jump on a trampoline, bike together, etc. On weeknights from late spring through early autumn, take advantage of how light it is after dinner to enjoy some outdoor family activities. The weekends are always a great time for family exercise.

• *Kids ages five to seven need close supervision to do homework. Older children can usually do their homework at a desk in their room. Even if kids have been in a homework club in their after-school care, you'll still need to check their homework.* (See page 39 to learn more about helping your child with homework.)

• In the evening, involve your child in helping prepare dinner and then eat together whenever possible. After a day apart, reconnecting as a family is very valuable.

• *Get into the habit of spending evenings with your children instead of catching up on work. If we have more work to do, it's best if we do it after our kids' bedtime.* That way, we're not pulled in so many directions during the time the family can be together. *Time together with us is better for our kids than screen time or other solitary time.* Our kids benefit from our more meaningful, individualized or family attention after being a member of a group all day. *When we can't find a way to switch gears from work to our kids, they will often dawdle, ignore us, or argue with us—just to get our attention. In contrast, time together* can fulfill everyone's emotional needs, and it builds the kind of closeness that enables children to more willingly accept our rules, guidance and values.

Bedtime and Sleep Routines

• *Children should have the same bedtime each night* so their bodies are tired at that time, and they can easily fall asleep. Parents need to start the bedtime process also at a regular time every evening. Four- to nine-years-olds need 10-11 hours of sleep each night, with the amount gradually diminishing during these years.

• *Beginning about 45 minutes before you want your child to fall asleep, the usual routines are: toy and project pick-up followed by a bath or shower, pajamas, teeth brushing, toileting, and then into bed for the rest of the bedtime routine*. Children up to about seven years old really enjoy and can relax in their **baths** which makes them very beneficial. Older than seven, most kids are fine with showers. Usually, we're with our kids during these pre-bed steps until they're at least seven years old.

• The rest of the routine usually includes stories and chatting for our four- to nine-year-olds. (Children who are learning to read will relax more when they're read to at bedtime, but if your child wants to read to you, of course, you should let her.) Set a consistent book limit or time limit on reading to your children or they may fall asleep too late.

• *Four- to nine-year-olds should be able to fall asleep on their own and sleep through the night—except for nightmares or illness. If you regularly stay with them until they fall asleep, then they may rely on you to get them back to sleep when they wake up about every three hours during light-sleep stages.* That's not helpful for you or them.

• Your preschool child may not be able to fall asleep at 8:00 or 8:30 if she is still taking a nap at school. See if you can get the school to allow your child to play instead of napping, or at least be able to sit up on her cot and play with quiet toys from home or school.

• At home, many children still want their stuffed animals. Night lights are important to some children. Some kids want to read by themselves for a little while after you've left their room. **Make sure there is a set time for lights out and that you enforce it.**

• About 80% of kids in this age range can go through most of the night (about 10 hours) without getting up to use the toilet due to the natural presence of ADH, the anti-diuretic hormone that decreases urine production in the evening. Try not to give them protein-rich food after dinner, such as milk or yogurt, because this type of food puts pressure on the kidneys and creates the need to urinate.

When we maintain regular routines for our kids, including consistent steps for getting ready for school, meal times, homework, TV and screen time, toy pick-up, bathing, and bedtime, there will be less pushback (limit-testing), which is something desired by all parents.

> *When your children are doing a lot of limit-testing, and you feel that you are giving in too often, a useful guideline is to ask yourself at the end of an incident, "What did my child learn from this? Did she learn that we didn't mean what we said?" If she did, she'll continue to push this and other limits in the future. It's much better parenting if she learned that we meant what we said, that we have good reasons behind our rules and, therefore, we are "respect-worthy."*

Have Your Four- to Nine-Year-Olds Learn to Do What's Age-Appropriate

This section is about making sure our kids learn to do what they are capable of and should be doing for themselves such as picking up their toys and dirty laundry; selecting their clothes and dressing themselves; bathing themselves; clearing their plates; wiping themselves after a poop; flushing the toilet; and carrying their backpacks. **Busy parents know it's faster if we do these things for our children—so we tend to do too many of these things for them. The problem with that is we need to teach our children to do what they are capable of.** Each year, there are more things that our children need to learn to do for themselves. We want our kids to become increasingly more capable and independent. *If we treat our children like they're younger by doing too much for them, then they are likely to resist doing these and other age-appropriate things*. We and their teachers will get frustrated that they're doing too little for themselves.

Additionally, our kids will begin to notice that their classmates can easily do many things that they don't do. Pre-kindergarteners will see that their classmates pick up toys, flush the toilet, carry their backpacks, etc. Elementary school children will notice that their classmates put away all their materials, tie their shoes, get right to work, and don't have to be reminded over and over by the teacher to finish a task. *If a child isn't expected to do age-appropriate things at home, he is likely to feel less sure of himself in his classroom because his peers do those things easily and because his teachers will be less than happy with him.* As you look at the list of expectations and routines (see page 31), consider doing the initial teaching of your kids on the weekends when there's more time and when you and your children are more relaxed. It's important, however, that your expectations become daily requirements.

It's useful to know that children typically want to become more capable in many ways, almost every day, so spending time teaching your kids how to clear their plates, put away toys, and the many other things such as not interrupting when others are talking, is not a punishment. *It's actually useful parent and child together-time, and it's part of how we help our kids become competent and, therefore, confident.*

What Do You and Your Children Need from Each Other at the End of the Day?

At the end of the school day, your child needs some individual attention from you. *However, when you first see her, make sure you're not overdoing the questions about her day. Many children don't like the questions we ask such as,* "How was your day?" (to which many kids will respond with a simple "fine" or "good"), or "Did you have a good day?" (to which many just say "uh huh"). *It can feel like a lot of pressure to our kids when we bombard them with questions such as,* "What happened today?", "What did you learn?", "Did you listen to your teacher?", "Who did you play with?", "Did you eat your whole lunch?", "What did you do in after-school care today?", etc.

There are *some children* who want to share everything with you right away, *but most don't*. They have spent their day doing what their teachers have told them to do. They also have been under pressure, especially time pressure. Throughout the day, teachers tend to say things such as, "You have two more (or five more) minutes to finish this." *So children typically just want to relax in your car or while walking home with you, and they really don't like an inquisition.*

Listen to see if your child has something she wants to talk about. (It may not be about school.) If your child doesn't begin talking about her day, then you can model how to begin a conversation by telling her something interesting that happened to you that day. *You should also teach her to ask you about your day.* (This helps her learn to be more considerate in her relationship with you and others.)

As parents, we love to hear lots of detail from our children especially about the things that worry us the most about them. *If we don't pressure our kids when we first see them, it's likely that they'll tell us what has happened as the rest of the day and evening unfolds.* Often, they tell us what we wanted to know, but maybe not everything we wanted to know. That's fine. Hearing about their day is more likely if you spend time with your child. *Bedtime chats are the most common time children tell us a lot.*

Once we're at home with our kids, we need them to do several things. We want our kids to bring all of their things in from the car and put them away. They may need to change their clothes. Kids need to wash their hands even if they don't need to use the toilet. They also need to have some free time and a snack unless it's close to dinner time. *They should have a routine that enables homework (which usually starts in the First Grade) to be done or checked as soon as possible.* (The later in the day that homework is done, the harder it is to do because kids can get very tired). If there's enough regularity in the evenings, consider working with your children on a schedule that they can have some 'say' about—just like the one discussed on page 31 about the morning tasks.

Children need a parent—even if it's just one—to be at the table with them for dinner. We should eat with, not just sit with, our children—even if we just eat a little salad or soup because we may be going to eat the rest of our meal with our spouse after our children go to sleep. Children need positive and social associations to eating. Eating shouldn't be something that our kids or we do fast just to fill our stomachs and be done.

Talking about something from everyone's day is very useful. These conversations should be more than just listing the best and worst (e.g., the 'roses and thorns') of each person's day because those are not conversation starters and they are very limited in detail. *Children and parents relaxing together and hearing about one another's day is a meaningful way to start to bring the day to an end as well as to understand one another better and build family closeness.*

Even doing chores together can be fun and benefit the whole family. *Most of our children would enjoy cooking with us; some would enjoy doing other household chores with us, including setting the table, doing dishes and*

kitchen clean-up, helping with the laundry, dumping garbage, etc. This is a useful way to spend time — if we do these tasks together.

Children should be able to do some activities of their choice in the evening—playing with their favorite building materials (Legos, Magna-Tiles, etc.), their crafts materials, imaginary play with their dolls, stuffed animals, etc. Parents should try to find some time to play with their kids. *If you're too tired to play with your children, then you can say, "I don't want to play right now, but I'm going to sit with you because I want to be with you."* Many children are quite satisfied with that as long as we actually pay attention to what they're doing and we don't use any of our electronic devices. **When we're on the computer, phone, etc., it looks to our children as if we're unavailable to them.**

Children may want some alone time but shouldn't be on their own for most of the evening. In addition to, or instead of, playing with your kids, you and your kids can look up information or do projects together. Making plans for future activities and outings is also valuable. (If you're trying to figure out what types of projects to do with your kids, it's very easy to do an internet search that includes your child's age and/or interests.)

At bedtime, read to your child. Have a consistent rule, either one or two picture books or one chapter or two. *That way, bedtime stories don't become all about negotiating. Remember to allow time for those valuable bedside chats, because that's usually the time our children have a great deal to tell us.*

If we can adhere to a well-thought-out evening routine (e.g., picking up toys, bathing, toilet, teeth and stories in bed) that begins at a set time—usually about 7:30 PM—

then we should be able to get back to our work at about 8:30 or 9:00 PM at the latest, rather than trying to squeeze it in during the time we're with our children. This requires a lot of self-discipline on our part. Just remember, we're doing this for the well-being of our children—their behavioral, emotional, and social development, *and* for us to benefit from having fun and recharging time with our kids.

• SECTION THREE •
USEFUL PARENTING BASICS

1. Try Not to Give Your Children Too Much Say or Too Much Control—Too Young

It's common for children to want to have their way and refuse to do what you tell them. This is called limit-testing or limit-pushing. We're supposed to teach our children that they can't just have things their way whenever they want. *Currently, there is a popular parenting approach with the presumed goal of building children's self-esteem. This approach says that we should give our children a lot of say, choice, and control as young as possible. However, this method is not working well because it tells us to encourage our children to make decisions they don't yet have the life experience or reasoning skills to make.* This method is making it harder for us to get our children to do what we ask. Letting four- to seven-year-olds choose the restaurant, or the order of the stores you will be shopping in at the mall, causes them to believe they should have a great deal of decision-making influence in the family. *Then they want to control more and more decisions. Children who have been given too much say before they're able to make good decisions often become very angry when we don't let them have their way. Some eight- and nine-year-olds can give us GOOD reasons for their views.* If they can, then they should be allowed to have some influence on family decisions. And as our children get older and develop more thoughtful reasons, we can give them more say.

When children have been given too much say too soon, many become resistant to listening to us and to others such as their teachers. This can also easily affect their social skills as they can expect to be the boss of their peers. Not many children want friends who are very bossy. *If you notice that your child expects to have equal or greater say than you do, consider using the guideline that your child should have some experience making decisions but only those that affect him* (e.g., choosing which kind of fruit he eats, which color shirt he wears, which toys he plays with, etc.). When your child insists on something that will affect others, including you, like what you're making for dinner, which mall the family is going to, etc., let him know that you are willing to listen to his reasons but that **this** will be a Mom/Dad **decision**. Tell **yourself** that this is because children are not old enough to decide this issue.

If your children tell **you** to go to time-out because you didn't listen to them, or tell **you**, "You're not the boss of me!" or "I'll only pick up my toys if you do what I say first," then you need more guidance on this issue. For detailed advice, see **Why Can't I Be the Boss of Me?** by this author.

2. Consequences: Which to Avoid, Which to Keep, and Two NEW Ones

Consequences are important tools that help us raise our children. It's nearly impossible to raise kids well without them. Consequences (which used to be called punishment) are supposed to teach our children to do what they should without us having to tell them over and over. Consequences teach our kids to think twice before they repeat the misbehavior. Of course, most of us wish we never had to punish our children. However, this part of parenting, although not enjoyable, is necessary.

A generation ago, there were five consequences. Three of them are no longer acceptable according to teachers, pediatricians, mental health professionals, and most parents. These are pain (e.g., spanking, slapping), fear (e.g., putting your child in a dark place or telling her that if she doesn't listen to you in the store, then you'll leave her there), and humiliation (e.g., embarrassing or demeaning your child). *These three consequences were used in the families that many of today's parents grew up in.* These three are now seen as unnecessarily harmful to our children, both physically and emotionally. *To replace these, there are three new, acceptable and valuable consequences, two of which will be described in detail here. In addition, there is an improved version of the still popular 'time-out' consequence. The other still acceptable consequence is taking away things or privileges ('take-aways').*

As parents, we need more than the two commonly used consequences ('time-out' and 'take-aways') so we can be more effective in teaching our children how to behave. Many parents become frustrated using only these two consequences especially when our children get to the age—usually about four—when they say things such as, "I like time-out," or "You can take away everything of mine! I don't care!" *Children usually say these things because they wish there were no consequences and they want us to think that these consequences don't affect them.*

Having five reasonable and acceptable consequences is much more valuable than only having two because which one we choose to use is less predictable to children, and therefore likely to be more effective. The two new consequences described here are: *'practicing better behavior'* and *'wasted time.'* The third new consequence is the empathy consequence and it enables you to have a total of five good consequences. For details on the empathy consequence, see **Why Can't I Be the Boss of Me?** by this author. *These new consequences also are educational because they teach our children useful life skills.*

New Consequence: 'Practicing Better Behavior'

Most commonly, when children do things they shouldn't, parents tell them not to do that again, often saying things such as, "Stop throwing the ball in the house. I've told you not to do that. Now, don't do it again! Do you understand?" or "You can't do that," while the child continues doing 'that.' *What works better than telling your child what not to do, is getting her to practice doing what she should do, typically practicing it three times in a row.* If your child is throwing the ball inside and, like most parents, you don't want her to do that, then help her figure out the **best outside locations** where she is allowed to throw the ball. Have her practice throwing it in those places. Then have her bring the ball back into the house and request that she **show** you what she should do with the ball when she finds it inside and wants to play with it. Have her practice doing this a few times. Also, have her tell you what she can say to herself to help remember not to throw the ball inside. (Believe it or not, this will only take 10 minutes.) *The best thing about this consequence is that your child will really remember what she should do with the ball instead of your having to repeat this rule for months or years.* If your child doesn't cooperate with practicing the better behavior, use the improved version of the time-out consequence (see page 37). Then, after the time-out, have her practice the better behavior.

There are many uses for the consequence of practicing better behavior. Here are some examples:

- **When children are rude**, saying things such as, "I know what I want to do and don't want to do—you don't!" or "You pick it up!" or "Get me my food!", **have your six- to nine-year-olds figure out a more diplomatic, respectful way to talk to you** (e.g., "When you're finished, would you make me a sandwich?"). If the words they choose are acceptable to us, then we should have them practice those words *two more times* so this *better behavior becomes internalized.* If your child seems too young (e.g., four or five years old) to be able to find a kinder way to talk to you, or if she is unwilling, then you can tell her what to say and have her practice it three times in a row. Listen to the words and the tone your child uses. We shouldn't accept silly or mocking voices. *Nor should we accept sarcasm or use it with our kids.* (Of course, there is the possibility that she and you might conclude that there's no kind way to say what she wants to, so it's best for her to tell herself not to say it at all.)

- **When children aren't making an effort to put away their toys,** you can set a timer for a few minutes and let them know if the toys aren't cleaned up by then, *that means they need a lot more practice, so you'll have to make another mess for them to clean up.* Then follow through. However, don't keep making more messes. *Instead use the 'new' time-out consequence if needed,* and then have her get back to this clean-up of the 'two messes.'

- **When children leave their other things out** (e.g., clothes, school books and papers, food wrappers, and plates, etc.), you can ask them a thought-provoking question such as, "What do you still need to do in this room?" and then have the child put the things away. (This type of question provides better learning and increased responsibility than if you just tell them what to pick up.) Then have her put the things back out and put them away twice more. Practicing better behavior enables her to remember better in the future because no one wants the tedium of this repetition.

Practicing better behavior is a much faster, more effective way for children to learn to behave better—and to internalize it rather than just 'telling' your child what she should not do time and again.

New Consequence: 'Wasted Time'

Children need to know that there will be a consequence when they have wasted a lot of our time by not doing what we asked. *If you have to tell your child something over and over or end up doing a lot of the job yourself, then that has wasted a lot of your time.*

For your four- to six-year-olds, and any of your older kids who still love to help you with your chores, tell them, *"Because so much of my time has been wasted, I'm behind in my chores. Now we won't be able to do _____* (mention something special or fun such as baking, playing a board game, or doing a project together—even if they didn't know about it) *that I had planned to do with you today. I hope that there will be better listening tomorrow so that we can do something special then."* It's very important not to say, "…because *you* wasted so much of my time…" because when children hear it phrased that way, they feel personally attacked and often verbally attack back (e.g., "No, you wasted *my* time!").

For the seven- and eight-year-olds, who view 'doing chores' as 'work,' tell them, *"So much of my time has been wasted that I'm behind with my chores so now you'll have to do my next chore."* Then pick something that takes at least 15 minutes and is relatively tedious, such as weeding, cleaning out the silverware drawer, or sorting all the socks in the family laundry. If they refuse to do the chore, let them know you'll have to give them a second chore because more of your time is being wasted. If they still refuse, you can use the 'take-away' consequence by not allowing a certain thing like dessert or a privilege. Or you could use the new 'time-out' and remind them they will still have to do the chore(s) after 'time-out' is over.

Improved Consequence: 'Time-out'

Time-out is usually useful for children up to about eight years old. *It allows parents to make the point that their child's behavior is so unacceptable (i.e., uncivilized or unsocialized) that she needs to be away from the rest of the family. Time-out should be in the child's bedroom with the door shut so she can't see or hear the rest of the family. It's best not to use time-out spots around the house such as standing against the wall, sitting on a chair, stairs, etc.* When we use these locations, our children usually do annoying things such as scooting along the wall or floor, or getting on and off the chair, going up and down the stairs, often making noise or calling out to us. Then we are forced to engage with them—which frustrates us more and defeats the purpose of *no involvement during time-out.*

Consider whether you need to remove some things from your child's room. Many five- to eight-year-olds are able to amuse themselves with their toys, books, etc., so time-out can lose its impact as a consequence. If that's a problem, you might choose a less interesting place, like your bedroom, a guest room, or the laundry room. Use one minute per year of age for the time-out (i.e., a five-minute time-out for a five-year-old). *Consider asking her a thought-provoking* question or two for her to ponder during time-out such as "What bothered me (the parent) about what you did?" or "What's a better way to behave the next time I ask you to…?" Expect an appropriate answer at the end of the time-out. If she's old enough, have her write a paragraph explaining to you why she misbehaved and what she should have done instead. **This gets your child to think about what she did while she is in time-out—something parents wish their kids would do, but we all know that they don't—unless they have an assignment!** You can also have her practice the better behavior after the time-out.

This updated set of five consequences (including the empathy consequence which is found in the book **Why Can't I Be The Boss Of Me?** by this author) **has the positive effect of getting our kids to learn to behave better. There is no set consequence to use for specific misbehaviors.** Try using these new and updated consequences until you're comfortable with all of them. Then you'll more easily be able to decide **at the moment** which is likely to be most effective. **These consequences are usually memorable and, therefore, effective for children without the negative effects of the now-discredited consequences of pain, fear, and humiliation.**

3. What To Do About Your Children's Screen Time?

The availability of electronic devices ("screens") is a significant dilemma for most of us in our relationship with our kids. Kids want screen time and lots of it. Screen time on devices such as tablets, smart phones, game consoles, and computers is an easy entertainment option for us to provide to our kids because it makes them happy and it fully occupies them. However, screen time can easily become addictive. We usually see our children getting **very angry when we remind them that their screen time is over for now or for the day.**

Of course, we want our kids to become computer savvy. Schools are now helping a lot with this. Most elementary schools offer computer labs. Many schools keep us informed on-line about what our children are learning. This enables us to follow-up at home with enhancing that learning.

However, we should pay attention to how much of our kids' screen time is pure entertainment. Often, the entertainment on screens is designed to engage a child so fully that it feels 'too good' and our kids are unwilling to stop. But as parents, we know there have to be real limits even though our children can get very mad at us when we impose those limits. **We should try to remember that it's very easy for there to be too much screen time.**

It helps to remember that too much screen time diminishes our kids' interest, skill, and comfort level with face-to-face interaction as well as their other indoor and outdoor activities. We want to make sure our children have plenty of in-person time with family and friends. *People relate more and better to others when they have enough meaningful face-to-face experience being with others.* These skills and experiences make for a much more emotionally fulfilled and successful life.

Almost all parents are struggling with how much time, and when, their kids should use these devices. **Here are some important screen time guidelines:**
- *We have to set limits on electronic devices because our children won't.*
- *If we are paying lots of attention to our own electronic devices, our children will want to do the same.*
- *Don't let your children have electronic devices, including television, in their bedrooms. Make sure they can't find ways to hide them there.* (The pull of these devices can cause some children to behave in ways they would never usually do.)
- *Limit your kids' electronic device use to the WEEKENDS. The maximum should be 30-60 minutes per weekend day for four- to six-year-olds, and one to two hours per weekend day for seven- to nine-year-olds.*
- *When your children's screen time is nearly over, give them a warning and mention some very interesting thing that they can look forward to doing.* Kids can't seem to think of anything else to do when we're trying to end their screen time other than wanting more of it.
- If your children can't stop demanding screen time, even with these limits, consider having none at all for a six month period. See if your children's behavior is better and if family life improves. **Then you might choose to extend the no screen time for another six months.**
- Remember that children need to play with real toys, do projects with real materials, use their imaginations, enjoy outside time and sports, and play face-to-face with friends, siblings, and us. **We should try hard to make that happen.**
- For helpful advice and support concerning screen

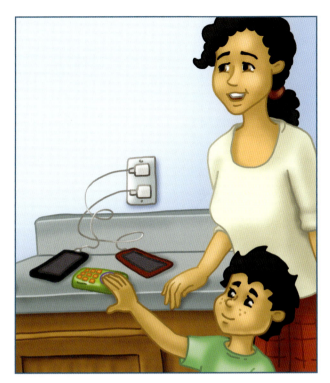

time, look up **Common Sense Media** and search for other parenting advice websites that can guide you concerning kids and screen time. (Of course, you and some of your like-minded friends will want to share what solutions you've all found.)

4. Dealing With Your Children's Homework

Many children resist doing homework. And many children (and even parents) feel homework is an intrusion into their after-school time. *It can be.* So it's useful for parents to learn to accept that the school regards homework as valuable. **When it comes to homework, parents are the middle-men between the teachers and our children, and we need to have the right attitude—one that will work for our kids even if homework is done at after-school care.**

Homework is usually given beginning in first grade, typically taking about 15 minutes each night and increasing grade-by-grade. More than a half-hour to one hour of homework each night for first and second graders would typically be considered too much. More than an hour a night for third graders is too much. If that's what's expected by your child's teacher, you may want to talk with the teacher or, if necessary, with the principal.

Children in first and second grade typically do homework with a parent sitting with them, usually at the 'kitchen table'. By third grade, most children have more self-discipline and can benefit from the independence of working at a desk in their room. After-school programs often have staff who will help supervise the homework. However, parents still need to check their child's homework. **Parents should also discuss with the teacher how much help to give. Helping with homework may be easier for us if we've done some volunteering in class, so we know how our children are being taught language arts, math, etc.**

Routines for homework are helpful. Children should not be overloaded with after-school activities. They need time for a snack and free-play in after-school care or at home, and they should have a goal of getting homework done before dinner, or as soon after dinner as possible. For many children, it's a good idea to help them decide which kind of homework to do first and what you should be "on standby" to assist with. **Some kids do better working on the harder parts first, and others need the opposite. Some children will need small breaks if there's lots of homework.**

It is likely disheartening or even infuriating to your child when you point out and make her fix every error. You could tell her that you see about 'X' number of places that need a second look. Then ask her how many of those she wants you to point out. **Putting this control in her hands can help a lot when you're delivering bad news.** You don't want her to feel you're fine with mistakes and sloppiness, but you also don't want her to have to do such extensive corrections that she hates doing homework. Additionally, if you have your child correct every error, there's the question of how the teacher will know where your child needs help. *If you don't point out more mistakes than each of your kids can handle, then over time, most kids will respond by being willing to correct more and more of their errors.* Ask the teacher how she suggests you handle it when you see mistakes or sloppy work in your child's finished homework. The teacher may have specific reasons for wanting or not wanting your child to correct every error you see in their homework.

5. Don't Let Your Children Stay Up Too Late— Have a Set Bedtime

Pay close attention to your child's *actual bedtime*. Pre-K and Kindergarten children need about 10½ to 11 hours of sleep, and first- through third-graders need about 10 to 10½ hours. **Children will be much more ready to fall asleep if they have a set bedtime seven days a week.** Naps for pre-K children (four- to five-year-olds) should be eliminated (or reduced) so the child can be tired enough to fall asleep by 8:00 PM or 8:30 PM. In fact, kids don't need regular naps after the age of four-and-a-half. Many children stop napping much younger than that. (If your child's preschool insists on children lying down for naps, talk to the preschool director about your child being able to play during that time or at least be able to sit up on his cot and play with quiet toys from home or school.)

It's useful to know that children need to go to sleep early enough that they wake up on their own in the morning. *Many adults believe that because they wake themselves with alarm clocks, that it's alright to do that for children. BUT IT'S NOT. Children are still physically growing and developing and need to be allowed to get the sleep their growth and development requires. This is the standard advice of pediatricians and it eliminates much of the resistance that tired children have in getting ready in the morning.*

Common bedtimes for children pre-K through third grade are 8:00 PM or 8:30 PM Children typically take about 10 minutes to fall asleep, not an hour. However, some children can take a long time to fall asleep. Problems falling asleep can be due to the following:
- If they've been rushed all day or all evening and are therefore stressed;
- If they didn't have enough time with you for bedtime stories and chats including telling you about their day and discussing their problems;
- If they've eaten too close to bedtime (i.e., within 1½ hours of dinner);
- If they didn't have enough heart-pounding exercise during the day; or
- If they're still napping at preschool.

Consider how you might help your child if any of those issues apply.

A regular bedtime for our children also helps us. Parents need to have enough time (e.g., 8:30 PM to 10:30 PM) when they can continue to work on the demands of their jobs, or meet some of their own needs as individuals or as a couple. We really need our time, and our kids really need their full night's sleep. *It's useful to know that adults usually need about three hours less sleep than our four- to nine-year-old children.*

6. How to See for Yourself What Your Children Are Experiencing at School

The most important way to understand what school is like for your child is to see it for yourself. You can do this by volunteering in her classroom monthly (or more often if possible). Public elementary schools usually encourage parent volunteers, but pre-schools typically don't. (If your child is a preschooler, you may want to stay an extra 10 or 15 minutes at drop-off if that doesn't create separation issues for your child.) Second best would be to go on several field trips with your child's class each year. *It's very valuable to do one or the other of these. Being in the classroom helps you know many things* such as your child's comfort level in the class, the atmosphere of the class, the approaches used by the teacher, what's expected of the children, and the dynamics of the kids, including who your child does and doesn't get along with. Time in the classroom also helps you get to know your child's teacher and her classmates.

You'll also see how your child is being taught academics (or pre-academics if she's in preschool), which is often different from when you were in school. If you volunteer in the classroom, your child's teacher *will have more of a chance to share very useful information about your child, such as how your child is doing academically, how she's doing socially, and anything else about what's happening at school—especially if you ask.* When you volunteer on a regular basis, you'll be able to monitor your child for any changes and get more frequent updates and advice from the teacher—all of which are extremely useful.

7. Consider What Your Children's Teachers Tell You

Teachers want us to know how our children are doing at school—especially if our children are having difficulties. Some of what teachers tell us may be difficult to hear. The teacher's goal is always for your child to have a successful school year. When talking with your child's preschool or elementary school teacher, remember that they are usually very experienced with children of your child's age. Teachers may want to give you feedback on your child's ability to listen to and follow directions, his pre-academic or academic performance, his behavior including social skills and emotional control, and any speech or motor difficulties. *Parent-teacher conferences are usually scheduled for October or November so teachers have enough time to understand and try to help your child with any issues they see before they meet with you. Teachers will want to alert you if they see problems that aren't improving, especially when they've tried to help your child over the preceding months but haven't yet been successful.* You can, of course, request a conference earlier in the school year for any concerns you have about how your child is doing.

As a parent, it can be difficult not to be *defensive or even in denial about some of the things our children's teachers tell us.* When you meet with the teacher, have your questions ready, listen to her, and take notes. If there are concerns, ask if she has suggestions for things you can do to help your child, or if she would recommend any additional services such as a tutor, a social skills group, a speech and language evaluation, or a mental health professional. (Many elementary schools provide some of these services.) *This input from your child's teacher can enable you to provide the extra help your child needs to make the expected progress at school. If the meeting with the teacher was too short, request another meeting.* If you feel the teacher is not skilled or experienced enough for you to accept what she says, talk to your child's preschool director or elementary school principal and then decide what to do.

• SECTION FOUR •
FINDING THE RIGHT SCHOOL AND THE RIGHT WORK SCHEDULE FOR YOUR FAMILY

Finding Quality Schools and After-School Care

Our four- to nine-year-olds spend most of their weekdays in pre-kindergarten or elementary school. *As parents, we want to check out the schools our children are likely to attend.* Looking at the school's website is usually the first step. Talking with the school's director or principal is usually the next step in learning about a school. *Observing a class in action is the third step and is the best indicator of the curriculum and the skill of the teachers your child will have. While observing a class, notice how the children are spending their time and how the teacher(s) handles any problems with the children.* Talking with other parents whose children attend the school can also be very helpful in your decision making. *If you're not sure what to look for when observing a class*, read the National Association for the Education of Young Children's very valuable book titled *Developmentally Appropriate Practice in Early Childhood Programs Serving Children from Birth through Age 8* by Carol Copple and Sue Bredekamp, particularly the one published in 2010. This book explains how to determine if what you're observing at the prospective school are good enough methods of educating and caring for children.

For elementary school children, we should also look at any after-school programs our kids might attend. Make sure you observe the program before you enroll your child. It should include indoor and outdoor free play, some organized activities, snack time, and crafts. Some programs for elementary school children may offer homework assistance. *As parents, we want experienced, organized, attentive, caring, firm enough adults in charge of our children in their school and after-school programs.*

You might also consider any specific activities you want your children to participate in such as sports, dance, music, art, science, other languages, etc. Many preschools and elementary schools now provide at least some of these special interest options because we usually can't leave work in the mid-afternoon to take our children to these activities.

Other options for after-school care include relatives, usually grandparents, as well as nannies, au pairs, and sitters. For all of these people, including grandparents, you will want to get as much consistency as possible between your parenting approach and their childcare style. Talk with the prospective caregiver about your parenting approach. If possible, observe your children with them so you can try to resolve any potential issues or concerns including differences between your parenting approach and their caregiving style. Make sure they also know the activities you want your children to do, as well as your rules for such things as screen time, chores, and friends they can be with. *It's also very helpful for your children to be with you as you explain the house rules to the caregiver. Then your children are less likely to try to get the caregiver to give in to their limit-pushing.*

Before you make any final decisions, take some time to discuss these choices with your spouse. Hearing each other's views is helpful and makes you more allied in your parenting partnership (i.e., *getting on 'the same page'*). Discussions with your spouse about your child's school and other regular activities will make it clearer to each of you what to expect, and result in less blaming of each other if difficulties arise in your child's education or after-school care.

Other Work Schedules That Can Ease Your Parenting

For many of us, full-time jobs seem to be more than full time. We already know we must have serious limits on how late we stay at work. We want to bring enough skill and focus to our career *and* to our parenting. We hope to do a good enough job of raising our children so they can have satisfying lives and make their useful contribution to the world.

So what other options might there be for the hours we work?
- Do we want to consider taking a position that is less demanding, less travel, less management of others— *just for the most critical years of child raising, which are usually the toddler to early teen years?*
- Do we want to have one of us start and end his job earlier in the day and the other start and end her job later in the day, so that our children don't need to be in school and childcare from 8:00 AM to 6:00 PM?
- Could each of us leave work earlier one or two times a week so our children can be picked up by 4:00 PM, and then we catch up on our work after the children are asleep?
- Could one of us work three-quarters time, so our work day is completed by 3:00 or 4:00 PM every day, as is seen in a few other countries?
- Could we work from home, either full-time or part-time, which would save commuting time and allow us to see more of our kids before and after their school day?

Depending on the type of work you do, you may have a few of these options. Each year, take a fresh look at what your kids seem to need from you and reconsider if it's reasonable for you or your spouse to adjust either of your working schedules.

• SECTION FIVE •
IMPORTANT VALUES WE WANT TO TEACH OUR CHILDREN AND HOW TO DO IT

Every parent wants their children to grow up with good values. *Values become the foundation of our kid's important life-long guidelines and beliefs.* You are likely working on some of these already. *Here are four of the most useful values.* Decide which ones you want to learn more about and start there. You still have many years to teach your children your values, and ages four to nine are the perfect time to work on these.

1. How Our Kids Can Accept That They Can't Have Everything They Want

Almost every day, most of our children see or hear about things or privileges that sound so good that they want to have them right now. As adults, we can relate to that. *Although there have been many things or experiences in our lives that we have wanted, we've learned that we can't have everything that appeals to us even when it seems we can't do without it. Now we have to teach that to our children.*

If you find your children 'wanting everything,' it's necessary to start having conversations with them about the times that you really wanted something and couldn't have it. Explain **why your parents said no to you** when you were a child. Describe how you felt about that experience and how you coped with the disappointment. **Don't make it sound easy!** Your children may bring up the issue of it 'not being fair' that other kids have things and experiences that they don't have. **Talk to them about how and why different parents make the kind of decisions they do for their children**. For example, you can tell them that if kids are given whatever they want, they get spoiled. They don't learn to work hard to earn things and they get mad a lot when they can't have something they want. And that's why you don't say yes to whatever they want.

Let them know that even as an adult, there are still times you want something that you could buy but shouldn't. **Share with them what you now tell yourself so you don't feel deprived, sad, or angry.** Make sure that your children know that there will be times when they feel frustrated or disappointed because a decision seems unfair. **Explain that how much we let it bother us depends on what we say to ourselves—this is called 'self-talk.' No one can have everything they want**. Explain how they can start thinking about something they *can* have or something they *can* do to get over their annoyance. Describe what's good about being able to handle disappointment (e.g., how you feel proud of yourself because you're not getting sad or mad).

However, you'll still need to deal with your children's demands about getting what they want. **Explain to them that although you're willing to listen to what they want, you'll need to make the final 'yes or no' decision**. This way your kids know from the beginning that you may say 'no.' When parents say, "*I'm listening* to what you want to tell me," many children **believe that means we will say 'yes' to them. Then they feel very let down and angry when we say 'no.'**

When your child says, "I really, really, really want THAT!" you have the opportunity to help her become a discerning consumer. Here are some steps for doing that (note that some of these steps may require shopping at a local store rather than online):
- Help your child become aware of whether she already has something similar.
- Teach your child how to know if the item is made well enough that it will last.
- Help your child find the price of the item and show her how to compare that item to similar products.
- Tell your child how much, if anything, you'll contribute to the purchase.
- If they still want to have the item, ask them to explain why.
- Tell them your decision (to buy or not buy it) and your reasons.

When dealing with this issue, it can be very useful if our children have ways to earn money so that they better understand the effort it takes to get things. The best way for our four- to nine-year-olds to earn money is by being more helpful at home. This way you can decide how much they can earn for specific jobs. **By the time your children are five or older, they can have regular chores that help your family such as setting the table, doing dishes, helping with laundry, vacuuming, dumping garbage, etc.** (*These chores are things they do for the family. They are different from self-care* — such as picking up their toys, brushing their teeth, taking a bath. **These are what they need to do and shouldn't be paid to do them**.) Discuss the possible age-appropriate chores with them, and tell them how much allowance you will give them each week for doing those chores. You and each of your children can post a list of their regular 'help the family' chores to be done each day of the week. You, your child, or both of you can check off the chores as they are completed. (Post a new copy each week.) **A portion of their allowance should be deducted for each chore they didn't do.** (Let your children know how much they have earned each week. You can keep the tally, or you can give them their allowance to be put in their 'piggy' bank.) Consider setting rules for how they can use their weekly allowance, such as spending one-third, saving one-third, and giving one-third to charity, or some other variation. **Any spending they do has to be with your approval until they are at least eight years old so they have made sufficient progress in becoming a good consumer.**

To help a child accept that "life is not horrible" when

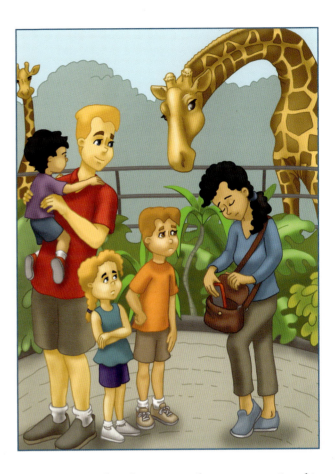

they don't get what they want right away, try using this useful type of a Wish List. This list should have space for only five items for four- to six-year-olds, and space for only ten items for the seven- to nine-year-olds. **If what your child wants meets your criteria (including its usefulness and cost) to be worth considering, it can go on the list. When the five- or ten-item list is full, nothing else can go on the list until your child decides which item to remove. This step is critical because it helps children realize that something they recently wanted so badly doesn't mean that much to them now**. That's important in children learning to say no to themselves so they can develop reasonable impulse control as a consumer.

When should we let them buy the things that continue to remain on their Wish List? Consider allowing your child to make her purchases on birthdays, holidays, or when she's earned enough money that, along with your possible financial contribution, she has enough to make the purchase. The main goal of the Wish List is to **make it easier for our kids to say 'no' to themselves and avoid buying things that they truly won't be glad they got…the next day, the next week, or ever.**

2. Helping Our Children Deal with Their Frustration and Anger

Everyone has feelings that are difficult to deal with—anger, sadness, and anxiety are the most common. **For most people, anger is the most difficult feeling because it seems we're at odds with the world. We may have trouble calming down. We can later regret how we behaved. And, less well known is that it's harmful to our bodies when we get very angry too often.**

Anger often starts as frustration, and if we can't handle frustration, we can easily become angry. So to help your child with anger, make sure he's not being overly protected by you or others from experiencing common, natural frustrations. Examples of shielding your child from common frustrations include — when you've told him that soon it will be time to leave the park and he doesn't want to, so you decide to stay longer *or* you let him talk you into having the seat he wants at the kitchen table, at the expense of the rest of the family. *Or,* just because he demands it, you give him back a privilege or something that you had previously taken away.

Frustrations are common in everyone's **daily** life. **If your child is having meltdowns when things don't go his way, think about your parenting and your spouse's to make sure you haven't been giving in too much.** If your children have been allowed to have their way too often, they can easily become angry at home, or with friends, and even with teachers.

Whether or not you find the answer when you think about your parenting, you still need to try to help your children modulate their anger by teaching them good self-talk. *Too often, children who can't control their anger have poor self-talk such as telling themselves things like "That's not fair!" or "Mom and dad should have let me go first!" or "My parents are just mean!"* These ways of talking to oneself cause children to become angrier and angrier and then they are more likely to lose control.

You can begin teaching good self-talk by sharing with your child some issues (that have nothing to do with the family) that have upset you. Tell him what you've said to yourself that made you angrier such as "that's not fair that the other person got the only one left on the shelf." Also tell him what you figured out to say to yourself that calmed you down such as, "I can wait until next week when they'll have more. It's no big deal." Then, on some days, just as you return home, tell your child of some upsetting situation that just happened, and say that **you** don't know how to calm **yourself** down. **Have him** suggest other things that you could say **to yourself**. It's easier for our kids to advise us how to calm down because they're not the ones who are angry at that moment. Giving you advice helps them learn what self-talk is and does.

It will be particularly useful to revisit some examples of situations that made your child angry a few days ago. That way, he's **not** likely to still be upset. Help him come up with ideas for calming self-talk. Expect to have to offer him suggestions if he seems stuck. **Make a point of continuing to share new examples of the helpful and unhelpful things you told yourself when you got angry. This can encourage your child to talk about his frustrations and anger and get better at using calming self-talk.**

3. Teach Your Children How to Choose Good Friends and to Be a Good Friend

It's useful to notice who our children are friendly with. We want to see if the children they spend time with are having a good influence on our child and vice versa. Examples of good influences would be children who treat others well (e.g., respectful toward adults and kind enough toward other kids), have a good sense of right and wrong, who don't need to either dominate our kids or to be dominated by them, who have interests in common with our children, who keep their word (especially when they're old enough, usually starting at six or seven years old), and who have fun being together.

If we're concerned about our children's choice of friends, then we will need to pay closer attention to how they interact with each other. Invite the other child to come over for a playdate and listen in as they play. To get to know her even better, invite the friend to join your family for an outing, provided that you'll be able to supervise the children closely. **Once children are in kindergarten, the visiting child's parents usually don't stay with their child at your home. This makes it easier for you to supervise and, as needed, correct both children's behavior.**

If your impression is that your child has friends who aren't good influences, it's time to teach your child what to look for in a friend. **Think about what you look for in your friends. Most of us like people who enjoy similar things, who are kind, fun, helpful, honest, and reliable.** Explain to your child that there are many ways for people to behave. Give her examples from various situations you've experienced. Ask if she can tell you about the qualities she likes in some of the kids she knows. **When she seems able to identify the qualities that are important to her, ask her what kids she does and doesn't especially like and why.**

Here are some of the problem signs to teach your children to watch for:
- If her 'friend' doesn't mean what she says (e.g., she ignores her after they had agreed to play together).
- If her 'friend' says unkind things about her to other children.
- If her 'friend' tries to get her in trouble by persuading her to do things that parents or teachers wouldn't want her to do including being mean to others, taking things, or lying.

Tell your child that when kids behave in any of these ways, they aren't being a good friend. Then ask her if she can identify some of the other kids who are likely to be 'good enough' friends.

We also want to teach our child how to be a good friend to others. Your child first learns how to be a good friend by the way you interact with her. Teach her to ask you questions about your day. This helps her learn to show interest in her friends and in you. You help her learn to be compassionate by noticing and talking to your child about her feelings, some of which surface when you're interacting with her, e.g., if she's sounding rude or sad, etc. Encourage her to take turns listening and talking. Be empathetic with her and praise her for being kind.

We want our children to help their friends, sometimes with advice but not by fighting battles for them. This can get children into trouble. And lastly, for our six- or seven-year-olds and older, explain how they should be able to be trusted with things they know about their friends that their friends wouldn't want to be shared. (Give examples if you can.) Explain to your children why they should keep these types of things private from other kids but not from you.

If you're feeling unsure about how to teach your children better social skills, read **Friends Forever** by Fred Frankel, Ph.D., published 2010; and **I Want to Make Friends** by this author, published 2012.

4. How Your Kids Can Learn to Keep Their Word and Be Honest

Parents want their children to mean what they say. We often ask them to 'promise' to do something *or* not to do something again. It's useful to know that preschoolers are almost never able to keep promises, so there's little reason to extract 'promises' from them. Some five-year-olds, most six-year-olds, and all seven- to nine-year-olds should be able to keep their promises (i.e., do what they said they would), such as getting their homework done before dinner or cleaning up their room before bedtime. **Since you'll probably need to remind them, the indirect approach works best. Say to them**, "What were you going to get done before dinner?" or "There's something you promised to do before bedtime." **This helps them take responsibility sooner rather than you just telling them again what they promised to do.**

This indirect approach also works well when checking whether they have handled their daily responsibilities such as teeth brushing or putting away their toys. **Asking the direct question, "Did you brush your teeth?" makes it easy for them just to say 'yes' even though they haven't done what they said.** So a better question to ask is, "Have you **had a chance yet** to brush your teeth?" This **phrasing** makes it easier for them to admit that they haven't yet done what you asked. **Then they're more likely to start brushing their teeth or putting away their toys without having to cover up their lie.** Doing random checks also helps our kids do what they should.

However, there are many children whose lies are a much bigger issue. These include when he says things like, "I got that toy from my friend," when he didn't, or "I didn't throw those pebbles at that car, someone else did it," when he did. It also includes when teachers inform us that our child told them, "Mom and dad said I didn't have to turn in the project because we were away for the weekend," when we weren't. **When we see or hear these types of things, we need to take it seriously and do more investigation.**

We should start spending more time asking our kids for details about what happened. Ask why they said what they did. **Try not to ask why they lied. Offer multiple choices if needed** to help your child figure out why they said something that wasn't so. We want them to tell us: "I really wanted to have that toy," or "I didn't want to get sent to the principal's office." Children who aren't being truthful may have difficulty doing the right thing and then blame others so they don't get into trouble. Make sure you talk with their teacher about these issues.

Spending more time with our kids, having more conversations, and **having some one-on-one time, can help build up our kid's sense of self and their conscience so that making up things becomes less necessary for them.** Then try to determine whether these approaches are helping.

We don't want our kids to make themselves "feel better" by taking things that they shouldn't or telling lies to their friends or teachers in an attempt to make others envy them. **More attention from us can help them do the right thing more often.**

We want our kids to know that it's important to keep promises and to be honest. *It's helpful to notice whether we keep our promises to our children, and how we explain it to them when we can't.*

When your child is breaking promises or being dishonest, find some **individual time** for chatting during activities such as driving, cooking, or at bedtime. These are good times to approach your child's broken promises or dishonesty. *For six- to nine-year-olds, you can say, "I've noticed you said you didn't have any homework, but I got an e-mail from your teacher today, and she said you haven't turned in homework at all this week. Let's talk about why this is happening."* If your child has almost nothing to say, ask him a few questions such as, "Is the homework too hard?" "Is it too easy?" or ask "Are you too tired to do it?" "Are you leaving it where you can't find it?" "Do you feel that the teacher never looks at it?" *Go through this process slowly,* giving him time to seriously think about these choices. *Let him know what you think about the value of his having homework and his reasons for not wanting to do it.* Suggest some possible solutions and ask what he thinks he is willing to try to do to solve this problem.

Other issues you might need to discuss are his taking things that don't belong to him, including money, his making up stories and telling them to other people, his blaming others for things he did, etc. Try to be calm and caring. Be prepared to suggest possible reasons he might be having any of these problems. Try these types of conversations for a month or even two, to see if that helps, or whether you need to seek additional guidance probably from a mental health specialist.

• CONCLUSION •
WHAT'S DIFFERENT NOW FOR BOTH MOMS AND DADS?

Today's working moms are groundbreaking because *almost none of us had full-time working moms when we were growing up*, so the model of how to successfully work, be a good parent, *and* feel alright about the way we do both is not yet there for us. Just a generation ago, mothers waited until their youngest child was in kindergarten or even in first grade before they went to work (or back to work). Now it's very different.

Because today's working moms have had so few models, *moms are likely to have a harder time than dads in dealing with their conflicting feelings, especially experiencing guilt around short-changing their children and their jobs.* However, on the positive side, moms often feel more fulfilled because of the many choices of work that there are for them *and* in being able to be more than 'just a mom.'

In contrast, today's dads have had generation after generation of fathers who modeled how to successfully work while also being a dad. That expectation has not been the hard one for them. The challenge for today's dads is what is expected of them: namely sharing childcare and household chores with their spouse to a much greater extent than ever before. *Dads are now expected to be partners in parenting with moms,* even when the moms work part-time or aren't in the workforce. This means that dads are still expected to be successful at their jobs *and* need to find time to provide more care of their children than they did in the past.

As a result of these changes, both working moms and dads have more demands on them. *Dads may be getting more emotional fulfillment from the increased time they spend with their children, while moms may be more troubled about spending less time with the children despite their very positive feeling about doing more than just raising their children. Not enough time, however, is the big problem for both parents.* When there's not enough time, dads may feel that they're short-changing their jobs while moms may feel that they're short-changing their children. *Or both parents feel they're shortchanging their family and their jobs.*

It's important for both mom and dad to be able to talk together about these changes and how they each are affected by them. These are important and challenging issues in how our families and society are evolving. All parents want to make the best of the opportunities we have.

With the help of the children's story and the parent guidance in this book, it is hoped that both of you will be able to do an even better job with more confidence and less internal conflict. And that you will both be able to provide a quality life for your children that will enable them to have many opportunities for a satisfying future.

B. ANNYE ROTHENBERG, Ph.D., *author*, has been a Child and Parent Psychologist and a specialist in typical child rearing and development of children from babies through age 10 for more than 25 years. Her parenting psychology practice is in Redwood City, CA. **She is known for her home and school visits that enable her to understand the children and their parents more fully and provide very targeted guidance.** Dr. Rothenberg is a frequent speaker to parent groups. She has also been an adjunct clinical assistant professor of pediatrics at Stanford University School of Medicine and consults to pediatricians and teachers. She was the founder/director of the Child Rearing Parenting program in Palo Alto, CA, and is the author of the award-winning book *Parentmaking* (Banster Press, 1982, 1995) and other parent education books for parenting guidance professionals. Dr. Rothenberg is the author of the six books in this award-winning series for preschoolers, kindergartners, and their parents. Every book has a story for children and guidance for parents. The books are: *Mommy and Daddy Are Always Supposed To Say Yes…Aren't They?* (2007), *Why Do I Have To?* (2008), *I Like To Eat Treats* (2009), *I Don't Want To Go To The Toilet* (2011), *I Want To Make Friends* (2012), and *I'm Getting Ready For Kindergarten* (2013). Her new series is focused on elementary school children and their parents. *Why Can't I Be The Boss Of Me?* (2015) is the first in *this* new series. The second is this book, *Mom and Dad Are Always So Busy*. Dr. Rothenberg is the mother of one grown son, who is her pride and joy. Her website is *www.AnnyeRothenberg.com*.

BONNIE BRIGHT, *illustrator*, has been a professional illustrator of children's books for 15 years. She also illustrates and animates digital books, and was previously an art director, game artist, and animator during a 15-year educational computer game career. She has done 3-D artwork and animation for major movie websites, such as *Shrek* and *Kung Fu Panda*. Her illustrated books include *I Want To Make Friends, I'm Getting Ready For Kindergarten, The Tangle Tower, Surf Angel,* and *I Love You All The Time*. She is married, has two daughters, and lives in San Diego, California. Her website is *www.brightillustration.com*.

ACKNOWLEDGMENTS

The author is extremely grateful to **SuAnn and Kevin Kiser** for their continuing and outstanding critiques and collaboration on the children's story, their suggestions for the illustrations as well as the final editing of the parent section. **Cathleen O'Brien** has again shown her terrific creativity and talent in the book design she has created. We're so grateful for her continuing work on all of these books. **Bonnie Bright's** work as an illustrator continues to be the best as she makes the children's stories so realistic and meaningful for these young readers. **The author is very grateful to the many parents who shared their experiences and those of their children** in dealing with the challenges of being so busy and needing to make the most of their limited time. **Their stories were the inspiration for all that is in this book.**

This newest book by Dr. Rothenberg is a detailed and practical guide for busy working parents on how to juggle their commitments to their job and more importantly, **how to foster a meaningful connection with their children and nurture that relationship for many years to come.** *This book has many specifics for parents from how to talk to their children in a respectful, empathetic manner so their children will feel connected, to how to set the daily routine in the household so all family members can work together seamlessly. I strongly recommend this book to all busy parents — stay-at-home or working outside the home — and to all the professionals who guide them.*

— Emily Ting, M.D., Pediatrician and mother of three children, Redwood City, CA

Most of us are working longer hours than our parents did. Many of us are expected to be on-call 24/7 by employers. Add in the distractions of the 24-hour news cycle, the constant texts from friends, and the pull of social media — it's **no wonder kids feel like they aren't always our top priority.** *Dr. Rothenberg's book,* **Mom and Dad Are Always So Busy**, *gives important and practical answers to parents. There is a lot in this book about how to speak to kids about our busy schedules and how to make time to nurture our relationships with our kids.* **It's well worth the time to read it.**

— Sarah and David Adelman, parents of a seven-year-old daughter, Mountain View, CA

Be sure to read Dr. Annye Rothenberg's other *all-in-one* books
for preschoolers, school age children, and their parents

Mommy And Daddy Are Always Supposed To Say Yes...Aren't They?

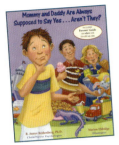

A STORY FOR CHILDREN— Alex insists that his parents should always let him have what he wants. In this story, he learns that even when Mom and Dad say no, they still love him ... a lot. INCLUDES A PARENT MANUAL—*Why don't children get the message about who's the parent?* How to give your child just enough say. How do you deal realistically with the differences between your parenting and your spouse's?

Why Do I Have To?

A STORY FOR CHILDREN—Sophie wonders why there are so many rules and why her parents want her to follow them. This story teaches the answers.   INCLUDES A PARENT MANUAL—Explains how preschoolers think, how to make it easier for your children to do what you ask, and the better and most effective consequences. *This manual clears up much of the conflicting advice that parents hear.*

I Like To Eat Treats

A STORY FOR CHILDREN—Jack wants to eat whatever he wants. His parents sucessfully teach him why everyone needs healthy foods.   INCLUDES A PARENT MANUAL —*Gives parents realistic guidance on common food questions. What to do about picky eaters. What about children who keep leaving the table.*

I Don't Want To Go To The Toilet

TWO STORIES FOR CHILDREN — Katie doesn't want to stop playing to go peepee in the toilet. Ben doesn't want to let his poop out in the toilet. *In two motivating and reassuring stories, the children successfully overcome their resistance.*   INCLUDES A PARENT MANUAL — Learn how to help your kids when they are uninterested, reluctant, and/or fearful.

I Want To Make Friends

A STORY FOR CHILDREN — Zachary thinks his ideas are the best. He learns how much that bothers the kids. *With help, he becomes a good friend.* INCLUDES A PARENT MANUAL — What to do if your child is bossy, annoying, aggressive. Or if they're shy and sensitive.

I'm Getting Ready For Kindergarten

A STORY FOR CHILDREN — Jillian has some worries about going to kindergarten. Through this story, she begins to feel ready for an exciting year.   INCLUDES A PARENT MANUAL — It has all of the important academic, social, and behavorial info parents need to best prepare their kids for kindergarten.

Why Can't I Be The Boss Of Me?

A STORY FOR CHILDREN — Ryan wants his way almost always. As his parents take charge, he realizes he's the *child* in the famiy.   INCLUDES A PARENT MANUAL — How much say to give your 5-to 8-year olds, how much to expect of them, and how to be in charge.

To order these books: visit www.PerfectingParentingPress.com where you can order online *or* call (810) 388-9500 (M-F 9-5 ET). These 40- to 48- page books are $9.95 each.
All these books are also available at www.Amazon.com